The Keys to Successful Healing

OTHER WORKS BY THIS AUTHOR

Words of Guidance by Son of White Cloud & the Wise Ones
Hihorse Publishing 1997
ISBN 0 909 223-68-8 (10) / 978-0-909223-68-7 (13)

Wisdom of the Australian Animals Book and Card Set
Hihorse Publishing 1997
ISBN 978-0-909223-76-2 (10) / 978-0-909223-76-2 (13)

Auz Astrology – The Australian Animal Zodiac
The Oracle Press 1999
ISBN 1 876494-14-X (10) / 978-1-876494-14-8 (13)

Inner Wisdom Guidance Cards
The Oracle Press 1999
ISBN 1 876494-20-4 (10) / 978-1-876494-20-9 (13)

Butterfly Kisses Inspirational Cards
The Oracle Press 1999
ISBN 1 876494-18-2 (10 / 978-1-876494-18-6 (13)

Inner Magic Cards
The Oracle Press 1999
ISBN 1 876494-28-X (10) / 978-1-876494-28-5 (13)

Australian Animal Tarot Deck
AGM AGMüller 2000
ISBN 3 905219-72-7 (10) / 978-3-905219-72-2 (13)

The Keys to Successful Healing
Auz Vizions 2025
ISBN 978-1-7638527-0-9 (paperback) / ISBN 978-1-7638527-1-6 (ebook)

The Keys to Successful Healing

Ann Williams-Fitzgerald PhD

Published by
Auz Vizions
14 Mary Street,
George Town, Tasmania, Australia 7253

Copyright © 2000 Ann Williams-Fitzgerald
The Three 'I's © 1994 Ann Williams-Fitzgerald

Text & Illustrations Ann Williams-Fitzgerald

First Published 2000 pdf
Revised Edition 2025

 A catalogue record for this book is available from the National Library of Australia

Williams-Fitzgerald, Ann.
The Keys to Successful Healing
ISBN   978-1-7638527-0-9 (paperback)
        978-1-7638527-1-6 (ebook)

1. SELF-HELP/Spiritual
2. PHILOSOPHY/Metaphysics
3. BODY MIND SPIRIT/Healing/Prayer & Spiritual

All rights reserved. No part of this publication may be reproduced, stored in a restricted system, transmitted in any form or by any means, electronic, mechanical, photocopying, recording or otherwise, without the prior written permission of the publisher.

ACKNOWLEDGEMENTS

I dedicate this book to Great Spirit, Sai Baba,
and my loving husband
Greg Fitzgerald,
who has always encouraged me with his unconditional love
and constant support.

I also dedicate this book to my son
Shane Fitzgerald,
who has challenged and inspired me.
Shane, you are my greatest teacher and I want you to
know how special and important you have always been to me.

CONTENTS

FOREWORD	7
TESTIMONIALS	8-9
PREFACE	10
WHAT IS SPIRITUAL HEALING	17
YOU CAN HEAL YOUR LIFE	24
NINE STEP PROCESS FOR MASTERING EMOTIONS	30
ACCEPTANCE IS THE ANSWER	38
FORGIVENESS KEEPS US HOOKED	58
THE KEYS TO SUCCESSFUL HEALING	64
BEGINNERS ADVICE TO HEALING	70
HEALING TOOLBOX	76
P.E.R.T. (Physio-Emotional Release Therapy)	77
SPIRITUAL MIND TREATMENT	83
THE THREE I's	86
CLOSURE	91
BIBLIOGRAPHY	94
ABOUT THE AUTHOR	95

FOREWORD
By
Bishop Charles Sommer
Madonna Ministry - USA

The avenues to successful healing are diverse varied and are done according to our beliefs in what works. Fundamental to all forms of healing is a love of life.

Dr Ann Williams-Fitzgerald's love for life is shown in her exuberance and in her work as a Spiritual Healer. Out of her own pain and suffering came forth the understanding of what brings about successful healing. Life is wrought with challenges that are opportunities to grow in spiritual awareness. Life is Spirit and acceptance of what seems to be the challenge can best be remedied by Spiritual Attunement. Life is Spirit and to be true to our essential nature is the most effective remedy.

Charles Sommer

Charles Sommer
Author
Licking Your Wounds
The Next Step With Spirit
Devorss Publication, Marina del Ray, CA USA

TESTIMONIAL
By
Kaye Murray

Dr Ann Williams-Fitzgerald PhD has covered the subject well, it is easy for the lay person to understand and precise. I agree with her, in regard to the word 'forgiving', people in many circumstances do find it hard to forgive what has happened to them and 'accept' is a good word to use, instead of 'forgiving'. The nine-step plan for mastering emotions is simple and straight to the point which people would appreciate when they are looking for immediate answers to their situations.

What Ann has covered is essential to our spiritual growth e.g. to know that we are responsible for what we do whether it is by thought, action or words, we predict our own future events and what happens to us. The hardest thing for people to let go of is fear:- fear of what people may think of us; fear of what people will say about us; and fear that people won't like us. If we remember that fear is false expectations appearing real, then we are well on the way to taking responsibility for our own lives.

The Keys to Successful Healing is a book that would be worth having on your bookshelf as a reference book whenever the need arose. I congratulate Ann on a book well done.

Kaye Murray
President
Australian Spiritual Healers Association Qld
(ASHA Qld Inc)
PO Box 1656
Caboolture Qld 4510

TESTIMONIAL
By
Minerva Press UK

Ann Williams-Fitzgerald's book *The Keys to Successful Healing*, is an engaging work in which Williams-Fitzgerald presents a framework for explaining and plan for dealing with our discontent.

This is an intelligently constructed piece of work: sensitive to the requirements of her readership, the author takes time to explain the foundations of spiritual healing and answer some commonly asked questions clearly, simply, and unambiguously, before presenting her own 'plan of action'.

This consists of a 'nine-step process for mastering emotions'; for it is gaining control of one's inner state rather than one's external environment that allows us to achieve satisfaction. And such control is possible, according to Dr Williams-Fitzgerald (who adopts a broadly cognitive approach): 'Emotions do not happen to you. Emotions are something you do,' That is, judgements that you make—consciously or otherwise—and can choose to reconsider.

Dr Williams-Fitzgerald author presents a lucid and convincing case. Doubtless, many readers would find this book extremely useful, and even those who disagree with the beliefs and contentions it expresses would find *The Keys to Successful Healing* stimulating. The written style is effective and appropriate. The prose is lucid and fluent and the sentences relatively simple in structure, yet Dr Williams-Fitzgerald's writing remains rich and textured. This is an ideal combination for a work of this nature.

PREFACE

I have written this book as a completion of my 'healing journey' and to share with you my readers that which I have come to know and that which I now teach.

Firstly, I feel that I must also share with you a little of me and who I am. Up until now I have been a very private person, even friends who have known me for many years, have not fully understood from where I have journeyed. So this then is my story to finding my "Keys to Successful Healing"...

My father was Polish by birth and came to Australia in March 1951 as a displaced person. He had survived five years in **Auschwitz, Dachau,** and **Natzweiler-Strutof** concentration camps (The Death Camps), before being liberated by the Allies in Europe. The horrors he must have seen and endured, I can only guess. He met and married my mother in 1952, and in 1953 I was born in New Norfolk, Tasmania.

My early memories of my childhood have slowly over the past ten years come back to me, they were so deeply buried for so many years because the pain was too great to allow the light in, but the light was needed for my healing.

I have fleeting memories of a baby brother, a sister, and a father. The majority of my memories are of a mother who beat me and abandoned me on more than one occasion, but also a father who sexually abused me. The last time I saw my father was in 1961 – he vanished out of my life, never to be spoken of again.

I grew up believing that my baby brother had died and that I was an only child. When I was 14 years old, suddenly I was told I had a 12-year-old sister who was coming to live with us. 'Us' being myself, my mother, and her boyfriend, who she later married. This sister had been abandoned when she was around one year old, with a family found from a newspaper advertisement and she was never collected until now.

My sister and I found it very hard to suddenly accept that we had a sister (each the other), as both of us had grown up as only children or so we thought! Times were difficult for us both. Our mother's fits of temper and emotional and physical abuse continued, she would throw knives, fire pokers or anything she could lay her hands on at us. I remember running and hiding under the bed whenever she would start to raise her voice and shout, because this meant I would be in the firing line. Even now, to this day, I can get uncontrollable shakes if someone starts shouting and yelling. My body instantly recalls the childhood abuse and wants to run and hide.

At 16 my life took another emotional turn, my mother decided that she would tell me that I was the product of rape and because of me, she **had to** marry my father. At 16 I found this shattering news—in 1994 I found this was in fact a lie—and for 25 years I carried the emotional burden of that untruth.

By the time I was 18 I moved out of home, I was married at 19 and had my son ten months later. My first marriage was doomed as I was dealing with so many ghosts from the past and abuse issues that I had not dealt with and certainly could not share. I could not bring myself to talk or share my past with anyone, least of all my first husband.

I guess in hindsight, my first marriage was a way for me to escape my childhood and my mother. My first marriage lasted two years and was over in 1974. I struggled raising a young child on my own for two years in Sydney before moving back to Tasmania.

By the time I was 25 I had produced my first lot of cancer. In 1978 I lost my first ovary to this dis-ease, but still I had not dealt with my abuse issues. Just buried them deeper and deeper. In 1980 I decided to leave Tasmania and I moved to North Queensland for a fresh start and a new life.

Within three years of losing my first ovary, I had a growth in my only remaining ovary, this too in 1981 was lost to cancer, one month before my second marriage. I was only 28.

Still I had not dealt with my abuse issues and again I could not bring myself to acknowledge the abuse or even talk to my second husband about my emotional, physical, and sexual abuse as a child. How does one talk about incest and deal with the associated issues it brings. I just buried it deeper and deeper again and stayed in denial. I now call this "putting dirt on top of the weeds" so you don't have to deal with the weeds in your garden.

Needless to say at this point, looking back in hindsight, that my second marriage was also doomed, no communication between us and my second husband was also dealing with his own issues and had a major drinking problem. This marriage also only lasted two years and was over in 1984.

Life seemed to run smoothly for the next few years, still I continued to push my issues down and refused to deal with them. Occasionally something would trigger off a remembrance of the deep dark memory.

In 1989 I had another battle with cancer – this time cervical, the battle continued till 1990. It was during a stay in hospital that the realisation hit me – and it hit like a ton of bricks! I was allowing parts of my body to be cut out, to be eaten away, to be destroyed by dis-ease – WHY?

Why... because I felt it was my fault and I was to blame for my father's abuse and my mother's abuse. I realised that I had to let the light in and pull those weeds out, not cover them up and bury them.

I needed to talk about these issues, I needed to share me with my partner and share my fears, my pain, and my abuse issues. I laid there, in my hospital bed at 1.00am in the morning and allowed the tears to flow, I allowed the realisation of what I had been doing all these years sink in, I acknowledged my pain, and I also came to the realisation that it was not my fault, I was the child in the situation not the adult. I allowed acceptance of the situation to develop and with that development I found release.

I was married in 1990 to my current husband Greg Fitzgerald and have finally found my "soulmate" the one I can share with and the one who has helped me to become whole again.

During the next few years, I found myself having 'flashbacks' of unpleasant memories from my childhood. Memories of being deserted and left with the nuns in a children's home **Resurrection House**, memories of being locked in a cupboard under stairs for days, memories of abuse from men in my mother's life. Memories of other unspeakable things. Slowly I started to piece together some of my past and reclaim myself, accept myself and started healing.

Then suddenly out of the blue in April 1994, I was contacted by my brother (the one, I was told died as a baby), and he was alive, married with a family and had been looking for his sisters for 10 years. What a shock, how could it be, it was unbelievable. The joy, the tears, the pain. He lived in Victoria – arrangements were quickly made and within a week I was on a plane winging my way to meet him and his family. The senseless loss of years together we had missed. Within a month we found out we had another sister.

This revelation dealt a huge shock – how could this be, what sort of mother abandons so many children? This time the anger surfaced along with the tears. Another trip was planned – this time to the High Country in the Snowy Mountain NSW to meet a younger sister. More joy, more tears, more pain, and more questions that would never receive answers from a woman who to this day denies it all.

By June 1994 I had produced a growth in my body again, but this time it was different. My brother had also produced cancer around the same time - his in his bowel, mine in my left breast. I had been down this road before and decided enough was enough – I had the tools and now it was up to me to use them. Within six weeks all signs of my cancer were gone, but unfortunately my brothers was a different matter.

With 18months of finding us, our brother died, again more tears and that question of why? My first book *Words of Guidance by Son of White Cloud* was dedicated to my brother and was my way of dealing with the grief of losing him.

This book *The Keys to Successful Healing* is dedicated to my completion of this healing journey and regaining my empowerment. If this book can help you, the reader, shed some light on your weeds or assists you to shine some light for yourself and or your clients, then all my journeying has been worth it.

I would not, if I could, change one day of my life as it makes me who I am today. It has given me the 'tools' for my empowerment and growth but only by **acceptance**.

Authors Note to Readers

I call God by many names, I encourage you to call God by any other name if that makes it clear and personal to you, such as: Spirit, Universe, The Creator, Great Spirit, Allah, Buddha, Quan Yin, Infinite Mind, the One, the Force, Light, The Source, Universal Mind, or any other term that feels real to you.

When I refer to healer or spiritual healer, this is meant as the practitioner or facilitator of the healing session taking place.

This book is about what I have come to know about my healing.

I

WHAT IS SPIRITUAL HEALING

*"We are what we repeatedly do.
Excellence then, is not an act, but a habit"*

What is Spiritual Healing or healing for that matter? A good question. Spiritual Healing is a very natural, gentle therapy treating the whole person. Healing means becoming **whole**. Becoming **whole** on all four levels – the best version of self. Those levels are the spiritual, emotional, mental, and physical.

We all have the potential to heal ourselves. Most people assume that healing only takes place in the physical. It is in the physical that we see the symptoms of dis-ease (the body out of ease) and illness but not the cause or source. The cause is usually found in the metaphysical and can be felt in the auric field years before it eventually comes through into the physical.

Spiritual Healing seeks the ***wholeness*** of the client by the power of unconditional Love, bringing spirit, mind and body into harmony and so releasing the body's own curative powers. It is therefore, primarily concerned with creating and maintaining a healthy balanced state on all these levels. It is the channelling of healing energies through the healer (*practitioner*) to the client. It revitalizes and relaxes the clients to enable their own resources to deal with illness or injury in the best possible way.

By 'attunement' – perhaps best described as a combination of empathy and intent – either in the presence of the client or at a distance – and by directing energy, usually through the hands, the healer (practitioner) seeks to supplement the depleted energy of the receiver, dealing with stress at whatever level it exists and releasing the body's own recuperative abilities to deal with the problem in the most effective way for the individual.

In *A Course in Miracles* Foundation of Inner Peace 1975, it states:

> "All disease comes from a state of unforgiveness" and "when ever we are ill, we need to look around to see who it is that we need to forgive".

Most physical illnesses have a mental or emotional issue, which may even stem back to childhood. Repressed negative emotions such as fear, anger, resentment, or hatred will eventually cause a physical illness of some sort to develop.

Spiritual Healing heals on all levels and often works on the cause of the illness first and will progress at the client's own pace. Spiritual Healing, regardless of what name you may give it i.e. Reiki; Seichim; Pranic Healing; Power of Prayer; Touch Healing; Ki Force; Tai Chi or laying on of hands, is simple, totally natural and is potentially unlimited.

Touch healing is described in the New Testament. Some form of the energy has been known in cultures worldwide, most spread by oral traditions, with beginnings long before the patriarchy. Tibet was the source of much of today's healing knowledge, both of touch healing and of the four bodies and the chakra system.

The Tibetan system of understanding the aura and energy bodies and of using them for healing has become universal. There are theories as to how this information, known also in Native America, India, Africa, Egypt, and China was discovered and taught in its beginnings. Who knows, maybe survivors of Atlantis, either directly or indirectly, developed the healing methods and taught it on several continents? There may have been an ancient worldwide communication telepathy network sharing information among cultures, information that was lost after the patriarchal invasions or the destruction and sinking of Atlantis.

Clients receiving healing tend to experience sensations of being re-energized or relaxed, 'pins and needles', heat or coolness, and pain coming to the surface and dispersing, indicating that the energies are indeed 'going to work'. Healing can be given for any illness, stress, or injury as a therapy, which is completely natural, has no side effects and is complementary to any other therapy.

It can be helpful in a wide range of physical and psychological conditions, sometimes to a remarkable degree, indeed, the medically diagnosed nature of the illness appears to be irrelevant to the outcome, and case histories range from the trivial to the terminal in which healing seems to have made an important, perhaps even over-riding, contribution to recovery. Aside from its value in relieving pain and restoring function, healing is also notable for initiating improvements in clients' attitudes and clarity of thought, and in their quality of life.

As a Spiritual Healer and Reiki Master some of the questions that I have found that are most frequently asked of me are:

1. Is it necessary to have faith?
2. Does Spiritual Healing or Reiki healing always work?
3. Can it do any harm?
4. How does the medical profession feel about Spiritual Healing?
5. Where does Spiritual Healing take place and is there any charge?

I would like to address these questions now in a bit more detail.

IS IT NECESSARY TO HAVE 'FAITH'?

It is totally unnecessary for the client to have 'Faith' in order for the healing process to take place (even pets respond well to healing). Nothing special is asked of the client except perhaps openness to anything that happens and a degree of trust in the healer (practitioner). An awareness of the need for change and the motivation to do so can also be helpful.

Those who undergo natural healing where the healer (practitioner) is present, experience a sense of peace and tranquillity, within this atmosphere healing is already taking place. So, for maximum benefit the client just has to relax and 'think well'. The healer (practitioner) may need to touch certain areas of the body, mainly the head, shoulders, or spinal region (but only with the prior permission of the client) and the client remains clothed. The client may also be given certain guidelines to promote healing between visits.

DOES SPIRITUAL HEALING ALWAYS WORK?

It is unusual for healing not to be helpful in some way. Sometimes one treatment is sufficient, but often several are needed, and the benefits emerge gradually. With some clients a successful healing outcome is obvious, but for some, change takes place at a more subtle level and sometimes in an unexpected way. Healing often helps with the speed and extent of recovery from serious illness and major surgery and from the effects of treatments such as chemotherapy and radiation therapy.
It works well with all forms of holistic medicine.

Usually clients feel more stable and relaxed, and often experience a beneficial change to their attitude to life, a situation which often arises in cases of terminal illness where healing brings serenity to the client and to the relatives and friends as well.

CAN IT DO ANY HARM?

Definitely not. There are rare occasions when the client may 'feel worse' before improving, but this is often a significant part of the healing process, signaling a release of stress, which may have gone unrecognized.

HEALING AND THE MEDICAL PROFESSION

There is a growing trend for healing to be given under the supervision of a doctor and healers' clients are always advised to contact their doctors about conditions, which may require medical attention. Healing is not a substitute or alternative: it works very successfully as a complement (adjunct) to other forms of treatment and a growing number of doctors practice Spiritual Healing or receive Spiritual Healing themselves.
I have among my clients three medical doctors who come to me for Spiritual Healing. Healing is officially listed as a therapy recognised by the National Health Service in UK and doctors are permitted by the General Medical Council in UK to refer patients for spiritual healing if they wish to do so.

Unfortunately that is not the case yet here in Australia. NFSH healers in the UK and Australia (ASHA) may also attend hospital in-patients who request their services.
Medical advice must always be followed since natural healing is a complementary treatment, which has no side effects and is beneficial to all - pets may also accept healing.

WHERE DOES SPIRITUAL HEALING TAKE PLACE AND IS THERE ANY CHARGE?

Healers work in their own and clients' homes, in the workplace, in doctors' surgeries, in hospitals, in healing and natural health centres, in fact almost anywhere a need for healing exists. Healing Centres are established throughout the globe to form part of the local community service for Spiritual Healing.

Many healers believe that healing should be freely available to all irrespective of their ability to pay. Other healers devote their life's work to Spiritual Healing and find they need to charge for their services. I advise my clients that the healing is free, but my time may cost $x amount of dollars per hour.

SOME FURTHER THOUGHTS

Spiritual healing penetrates the deepest levels of a person's being where many illnesses have their origin - stress, tension, and fatigue - so that symptoms disappear when the cause is revealed and removed. Changes in attitude and the quality of life often follow and continue the good work. The power of nature to enable us to help ourselves, recognised for thousands of years, has been overshadowed in modern times by the growing emphasis on technology, its benefits underestimated, under-utilised, and misunderstood. It is this power of nature which spiritual healers seek to tap, addressing illness and injury at its source and aiding recovery at all levels of the clients being.

Unfortunately, most of the medical profession address the symptoms of dis-ease and illness and not the cause or source of it. (Some may look deeper, Psychiatrists).

II

Review of Literature
YOU CAN HEAL YOUR LIFE

*"He who knows others is wise,
He who knows himself is enlightened"*

Disease does not bring pain. The pain of your soul brings disease. Pain is good because it gives you the idea that you need to look into yourself. Use the pain. We can not transmute or transcend anything we cannot feel.

We need to understand that we are a soul with a physical body—not a physical body with a soul—a spiritual being, energy, and that soul is the energy or the life force that keeps the cells of our body alive. If we are having trouble with our bodies, we need to go to our soul and see where we are going against our soul's plan in this lifetime. By changing that concept or the way we are thinking, our body will heal. In fact, if we are having trouble with our loved ones or our friends, our soul part is where we go to heal it.

This is how we grow spiritually and raise our level of consciousness to become one with all. Too many people think that spiritual growth is a race off the planet. The energy of death is present in the aura of this planet and those that love her cannot leave her at this moment. We need to love the earth's body as if it was our own because it is. We need to dedicate our life force to healing the planet. This is the reason for coming to this planet, to heal ourselves and our limitations and fears.

These fears, etc. stop us from experiencing the way we can use our skills and our full potential to manage the planet's resources responsibly; but our judgement of self and others cause these fears to suppress our expressions of joy.

Fear is a false god, and we do not need it.
We need to become fearless.

- F False
- E Expectation
- A Appearing
- R Real

We need to have faith in ourselves. Love ourselves unconditionally and not to be afraid to look inside.

All the things that go against us and create disharmony in our thinking are EMOTIONS, which are REACTIONS, and they are the way society has taught us to react to things. What other people tell us we ought to or should do. It is our intellect, our ego – our thinking mind and it likes to have control. It wants to control our life, but we need to police our thoughts, feelings and work out **what, when, where** and **why** of our true feelings.

FEELINGS are for ACTION.

When you follow your true feelings, you are doing what is best for you and you are in control of your own life.

Thoughts are energy and they are powerful.

We can use this power to work for ourselves and not against us, by changing our thoughts to heal our body. The pressures that an illness can give us can be termed 'good' because it will force us to do something for ourselves and change and learn from it.

Some so-called incurable diseases can be cured by simply changing the thoughts that have caused it because the cells in our bodies completely rejuvenate each seven years as we go into a new learning cycle. It may take time, but we can heal our bodies if we want to. There are a few people who do not want to change and heal their bodies. They will just need to do it next lifetime.

If you keep the big picture of you as a soul needing to keep evolving and learning from everything you do, you will not waste your time while here this lifetime.

Why be afraid of death when a soul never dies?
Our body is a vehicle for our soul.

To me the meaning of **d.e.a.t.h.** is:
D = Departing
E = Earth
A = and
T = Trekking
H = Home

A soul is energy, it was, it is, and it always will be. A soul enjoys life when it keeps evolving. We need continuous growth from learning about ourselves. It is the spiritual understanding of what we are doing in the physical that gives us balance. If we take a look at the yin yang symbol, we see equal amounts of black and white in this symbol. This is the symbol for harmony.

I believe that to have harmony we must have equal amounts of 'good and bad', day and night, black and white, positive, and negative. I do not mean bad in the sense of not good. I mean bad in the sense of our shadow side. Equal amounts of highs and lows in our life to have balance.

The left side of our bodies (the female side) has to do with our spiritual feelings and the right side of our bodies (the male side) has to do with our physical and material thinking.

Louise Hay states in **YOU CAN HEAL YOUR LIFE** 1984 that

> *"Life is really very simple. What we give out, we get back"* she also states that *"What we think about ourselves becomes the truth for us. I believe that everyone, myself included, is 100% responsible for everything in our lives, the best and the worst. Every thought we think is creating our future. Each one of us creates our experiences by our thoughts and our feelings. The thoughts we think and the words we speak create our experiences. We create the situation, and then we give our power away by blaming the other person for our frustration. No person, no place, and no thing has any power over us, for 'we' are the only thinkers in our mind. We create our experiences, our reality and everyone in it. When we create peace and harmony and balance in our minds, we will find it in our lives."*

It is our absolute need to look inside and find our purpose and know where we came from, what we are doing here and where we are going, then move into fulfilling our purpose and not waste our time here. Knowing your direction keeps you living in the present. Forget about being guilty of your past and stop worrying about your future.

All you need is to live in the "NOW" and just "BE" yourself. "BEINGNESS" is your key to your freedom and your one with all-ness.

The following is my understanding of the reasons to look inside so we can grow spiritually and raise our level of consciousness and heal our bodies.

- Becoming enlightened about who you really are, where you come from, and what you are doing here, and where you are going, and finding your purpose.
- Learning from everything you do.
- Healing limitations, fears and thoughts of guilt and suffering, so you can enjoy life.
- Being in control of your own energy and using your time wisely and not wasting it on trivia.
- Minding your own business and not controlling others.
- Working from 'The Three I's = Integrity, Intention & Intuition.
- Developing a 'live and let live' attitude or better still a 'love and let live' attitude.
- Having balance between your spiritual life and your physical and material life.

- ❖ Understanding yourself and removing any reaction you have been taught that stops you from being the free soul that you are.
- ❖ Getting back to being yourself into your feelings. Not letting your intellect or ego take over your life.
- ❖ Being at one with the universe and generally raising your level of consciousness with awareness.

Louise Hay states in **YOU CAN HEAL YOUR LIFE 1984** that

> *"We can change our attitude toward the past"* She goes on to state *"The past is over and done. We cannot change that now. Yet we can change our thoughts about the past. How foolish for us to PUNISH OURSELVES in the present moment because someone hurt us in the long ago past. I often say to people who have deep resentment patterns."*

> *"Please begin to dissolve the resentment now when it is relatively easy. Don't wait until you are under the threat of a surgeon's knife or on your death bed, when you may have to deal with panic too."*

> *"To release the past, we must be willing to forgive. We need to choose to release the past and forgive everyone, ourselves included. We may not know how to forgive and we may not want to forgive, but the very fact we say we are willing to forgive begins the healing process. It is imperative for our own healing that 'we' release the past and forgive everyone."*

III

Methods
THE NINE STEP PLAN FOR MASTERING EMOTIONS

This is my nine-step process for assisting my clients to the mastering of their emotions; I have found this to be extremely helpful with my clients.

Emotions do not happen to you. Emotions are something you do. Emotions are a goal-orientated activity. They are causes, not results. It may seem that an emotion is something, which happens to you as a result of another person's action or attitude, actually, it is an action you take expecting to produce a particular response or result.

The Nine Step Process is not for suppressing emotions. If your emotion is appropriate and serving you well, go ahead and express it. The Nine Step Process is for understanding your emotions and for being certain that this particular emotion is the appropriate action you wish to take for best results.

STEP I
Recognise your Moment of Decision

There is a particular moment when you decide that an emotional response is the action to take in a situation. In other words, recognise that, at that moment, you are having an emotional response. Denial is more common than we realise. When you don't want to admit that you are being affected, you may say 'I am not mad' or 'I am not jealous', or 'I am not irritable'. Catch the earliest moment of recognition, the onset of emotion, preceded by a thought.

STEP II
Describe the Emotion Honestly and Accurately

Instead of saying 'I am angry', say 'I am feeling selfish and want to manipulate him/her, and I don't like the way he/she is acting. I am feeling this way so they will notice how upset I am, and they will act differently'. In other words examine what you are feeling, and don't use socially acceptable labels such as 'anger', 'jealousy', 'depression' etc.

Describe your emotions as being socially unacceptable, which it is. It will help you realise that what you are doing is something that can be seen and recognised by others in a socially unacceptable manner and forms their impression of your action. When others see you expressing emotion, they know it is something you are doing. It is only when they are feeling emotion that they believe it is something that just happens 'to me', as if they were a victim.

STEP III
Accept Responsibility for Your Action

Instead of saying 'you hurt my feelings', notice that what really happened, is that you chose to feel hurt, in response to something 'they' did. You could have interpreted their action in another way, or you could choose to respond by feeling exactly as you most enjoy feeling without assuming that your feeling is cause/effect related to their action. You feel what you choose to feel. You should assume total responsibility for what you feel and express. What 'they' did may be very wrong, but that does not obligate you to feel a particular way in response to it. Be honest. Accept responsibility.

STEP IV
Identify the Catalyst Objectively

Ascertain the exact incident or communication that caused you to decide to respond with an emotional reaction. Describe as objectively as possible the catalyst of your action. This catalyst is what you need to call the 'cause' of your emotion.

STEP V
Identify the Cause

The real cause of your emotional action is a belief you hold about the catalyst. Because of your belief about the catalyst, you feel you must respond in a certain way to get a particular result or to rectify the situation. These beliefs are usually irrational and a result of the values of our parents and acquaintances in early life. When examined they may change.

STEP VI
Examine the Validity of The Belief

To identify your belief about the catalyst may very well be the most difficult step in the process. You have usually hidden these irrational beliefs in order to avoid responsibility for acting in a mature manner (that is, you avoid change). Now you must examine the validity of the belief. Is your belief about that catalyst rational, and is the emotion a valid response?

STEP VII
Identify Your Carrot [Result or Intent]

Your 'carrot' is the result you hope to get from your emotional action. A wife may express anger in order to get a word of appreciation for her work in preparing a meal. When the husband doesn't notice, she may become sullen and angry. What is her CARROT? At first, it was a simple compliment, which she wanted; now, however, she wants an apology and contrition (She wants more now for the extra trouble of expressing an emotional response).

STEP VIII
Determine the Cause/Effect Relationship between the Action and the Carrot

Is the action likely to produce the result you want? If not, what is the likely result of your action? Do you want to produce that result? Is your emotion working?

STEP IX
Select a More Appropriate Action

If the emotion/action you have taken does not work for you, if it makes you suffer and even then, does not produce the desired result, you may want to be aware of that cause/effect action when such a catalyst is presented. So by being true to ourselves, in the moment, we remain current with our emotions. The following is a nine-step program that metaphysical counsellors can use to assist their clients to unhook from the emotions.

NINE STEPS FOR MASTERING EMOTIONS
Exercise

1. Identify the emotion by its societal name, recognise and describe what it is doing to your body.

   ....

   ....

   ....

2. Describe the emotion.

   ....

   ....

   ....

3. Accept responsibility. 'They' didn't do it to me. At some level I chose to experience the emotion. I want to understand and choose a better response for me whether they change or not. Yes, or No? If you answer 'no', you have only completed a 'three' step.

   ....

   ....

   ....

4. The catalyst or event/story:
   Describe the **WHO, WHAT, WHEN, WHERE, WHY** and **HOW** your buttons have been pushed and take it back to an earlier event, as far back as possible (father/males, mother/females), when this emotion first came up. Listen to the self-talk and write the beliefs down under step 5.

   ....

   ....

   ....

5. The **Causes** for being upset. My beliefs about myself or about myself in the situation.
   a) the closer they come to the real emotion, the better this is a core belief.
   b) "I don't know" means: the computer or ego is blank. Ego is about to see something it doesn't want to see. Repeat what you just said and find out what the real belief is behind it; friends may help by brainstorming.

   ....

   ....

   ....

6. Does holding these beliefs make my life any more harmonious, peaceful, or beautiful?
   (Answer for each belief expressed under 5, put 'yes' or 'no' beside each belief)

   ....

   ....

   ....

7. What is my reward or carrot for this behaviour? Why did I choose such behaviour?
   (Usually some form of attention or a love substitute, do pity-parties make my life more harmonious, peaceful, or beautiful?)

   ....

   ....

   ....

8. a) What do I really want?
   (Unconditional love? Acceptance?)

   ....

   b) Does the emotion work to get me this?
   (Usually negative emotions get us the exact opposite of what we want.) Example: Jealousy drives a lover further away, instead of making greater attraction.
   Yes or **no**

   ....

9. What is a more appropriate response?
   What will get me what I want?

   ....

   ....

   ....

Develop positive affirmations to describe the state of mind or action you wish to experience in a similar situation (write on a separate sheet of paper).

Make **'grace'** replace 'karma' as soon as possible and start practicing affirmations. (Use **I am**, instead of I can, or I will). And do your new behaviour and responses with peace, joy, truth, happiness, and beauty!

Our thoughts create our reality, and we have to ability to choose what we focus on, and our words will empower (turbo boost) our thoughts. As we think so we become, it is part of universal law – what goes out will come back. Stop for a moment and think about what words you want to release out there into the Universe. The universe will not filter your words, that is your role before you send them out.

Remember your **words are powerful**, and your affirmations need **action** to empower them.

IV

Findings
ACCEPTANCE IS THE ANSWER

"I am forgiven, and I am Free"

"The road to freedom is through the doorway to forgiveness" Louise Hay states in **LOVE YOURSELF, HEAL YOUR LIFE 1990.** She goes on to state:

> " We may not know how to forgive, and we may not want to forgive; but if we are willing to forgive, we may begin the healing process. It is imperative for our own healing that we release the past and forgive everyone. This does not mean that I condone poor behaviour. I want to encourage the process of setting you free. Forgiveness mean's giving up, letting go. We understand our own pain so well. Yet, it is hard for most of us to understand someone's pain that has treated us badly. That person we need to forgive was also in pain. And they were only mirroring what we believed about ourselves. They were doing the best they could given the knowledge, understanding and awareness they possessed at the time"

I believe that we can change our attitude towards the past. It is over and done and cannot be changed. Yet we can change our thoughts about the past. How foolish for us to punish ourselves in the present moment because someone hurt us long ago. If we choose to believe that we are helpless victims and that all is hopeless, then the universe will support us in the belief. The universe will confirm our worst thoughts of ourselves.

If we choose to believe that we are responsible for our experiences, the good and the so-called bad, then we have the opportunity to outgrow the effects of the past. We can change and we can be free. We need to remember that thoughts are energy, and they are powerful.

> *It is your attitude, not your aptitude that determines your altitude.*

I feel that our existence on this planet has eight guidelines to follow:

1. **KNOW WHO YOU ARE**
   This is essential to you because you will have direction and purpose for why you are here to have the feeling that you belong.

2. **ONE WITH ALL**
   This is the feeling that you know you are one. One with all nature, minerals, plants, and animals. One with all humanity, one with the universe, one with yourself. Respect and love for one another, no matter how different, they are all you.

3. **LOVE OF SELF AND ACCEPTANCE OF SELF**
   This knowing that you are loved, and you are a powerful energy force radiating that love from your aura. By loving yourself first and accepting yourself, your glow attracts others to you, and they learn from your example.

4. **COMMUNICATION**
   This can be done verbally or nonverbally. Speaking our truths and listening to others brings about our learning. It is giving and receiving. Sharing our feelings. Communication with your inner Guidance is essential for you to understand your experiences and to understand others to communicate with humility.

5. **CREATION**
   This is bringing forth new ideas, which are never ending. There is always another or better way to do something. Know you can create your own destiny by your desire to manifest the best for yourself. You are the one who can decide what sort of life you want for yourself. It is your choice.

6. **DIRECTION**
   This is knowing your purpose for being here. When you know this, you make the best decision for you, and you take little notice of fears and limitations that could stop your Soul's plan.

7. **SENSITIVITY**
   This is living in the present moment (being real as I call it) and allowing your self to just BE. Listening to your inner, instead of just hearing. Seeing the big picture, instead of just looking. Perceiving feelings from the soul to soul like a radar system. This way you really understand and know what is happening and the words "I don't know" will never enter your head. We perceive far more from what we do not say than what is actually said in words.

8. **BOUNDARIES**
    It is important to set boundaries. They are about stating what we do and don't want, and our limits. It's important to remember that we're all responsible for setting our own boundaries and for how we respond to other people's behaviour. Sometimes, in order to maintain a boundary, we might need to leave a situation temporarily, or even permanently.

In various writings we are told that forgiveness will set us free. Well *I disagree*, as a survivor of physical, emotional, and sexual abuse I have found over the years, that forgiveness does not set you free. In fact, quite the opposite.

I believe that **forgiveness** is a **judgement** that keeps us **hooked** into the **pain**, the past and we need to release all judgements made by us.

Over the years I have had many counselling clients come to me who have spent years in counselling sessions with other counsellors who have told them that they must forgive and get over the past. These clients have found that they could work on releasing the past but still could not forgive. By trying to forgive as their counsellors instructed them, they were in fact putting themselves back into the raw wound of the past.

I feel it is God's place to forgive but our place to accept. Acceptance does not mean it's ok those things happened, but that we can accept that it happened and move on.

If we take a look at some exercises that Louise Hay is using in *YOU CAN HEAL YOUR LIFE 1984*, we will see how forgiveness is a judgement.

> "Exercise: Forgiveness
> Now we are ready to forgive. Do this exercise with a partner if you can, or do it out loud if you are alone. Sit quietly with your eyes closed and say, 'The person I need to forgive is_____ and I forgive you for_____.' Do this over and over. You will have many things to forgive some for and only one or two to forgive others for. If you have a partner, let them say to you, 'Thank you, I set you free now'. If you do not, then imagine the person you are forgiving saying it to you. Do this for at least five or ten minutes. Search your heart for the injustices you still carry. Then let them go. When you have cleared as much as you can for now, turn your attention to yourself. Say out loud to yourself, 'I forgive myself for_____'. Do this for another five minutes or so. These are powerful exercises and good to do at least once a week to clear out any remaining rubbish. Some experiences are easy to let go and some we have to chip away at, until suddenly one day they let go and dissolve."

If we look at that above exercise and take the judgement and blame of forgiveness out and replace it with the word **ACCEPTANCE**, we get the following exercises that do release you from the past. There is no judgement on you or on others from the past. Just freedom and release from all past issues.

Exercise: *ACCEPTANCE*

Now we are ready to **ACCEPT**. *Do this exercise with a partner if you can or do it out loud if you are alone.*

*Sit quietly with your eyes closed and say, 'The person I need to **accept** is_____and I **accept** you for_____'.*

*Do this over and over. You will have many things to **accept** some for and only one or two to **accept** others for. If you have a partner, let them say to you, 'Thank you, I set you free now'. If you do not, then imagine the person you are **accepting** saying it to you. Do this for at least five or ten minutes. Search your heart for any injustices you still carry. Then let them go. When you have cleared as much as you can for now, turn your attention to yourself. Say out loud to yourself, '**I love and accept myself just as I am**'. Do this for another five minutes or so. These are powerful exercises and good to do at least once a week to clear out any remaining rubbish and judgements. Some experiences are easy to let go and some we have to chip away at, until suddenly one day they let go and dissolve.*

By changing the above exercise we have effectively released the judgement and blame that was contained within the first exercise.

Louise Hay states in YOU CAN HEAL YOUR LIFE 1984

> *"I would add to that concept that the very person you find it hardest to forgive is the one YOU NEED TO LET GO OF THE MOST. Forgiveness means giving up, letting go. It has nothing to do with condoning behaviour. It's just letting the whole thing go. We do not have to know how to forgive. All we need to do is to be willing to forgive. The universe will take care of the hows. We understand our own pain so well. How hard it is for most of us to understand that they, whoever they are we need most to forgive, were also in pain. We need to understand that they were doing their best at the time"*

I **disagree** with Louise Hay's statement, regarding forgiveness is giving up and letting go, I feel it is hanging onto the past, not letting go of it.

Louise Hay also states

> *"When people come to me with a problem, I don't care what it is – poor health, lack of money, unfulfilling relationships, or stifled creativity – there is only one thing I ever work on, and that is LOVING THE SELF. I find that when we really love and accept and APPROVE OF OURSELVES EXACTLY AS WE ARE, then everything in life works. It's as if little miracles are everywhere. Our health improves, we attract more money, our relationships become much more fulfilling, and we begin to express ourselves in creative fulfilling ways. All this seems to happen without our even trying" "Self-approval and self-acceptance in the now are the main keys to positive changes in every area of our lives."*

I wholeheartedly **agree** with this and feel it is one of the most powerful statements made by Louise Hay in *YOU CAN HEAL YOUR LIFE, 1984.*

There are eight *'Points of Empowerment'* that I feel are very important for clients so they may begin their own work on self-acceptance and self-love. I have found these to be extremely powerful ways to effect change.

'Points of Empowerment'

"I believe in my own power to change"

"I give myself permission to learn"

It is not the people, places or things that are creating a problem for you; it is how you are 'reacting or perceiving' these life experiences. There is no such thing as a problem – only a situation that as yet you have not found a solution. Take responsibility for your own life. Do not give your power away. Learn to understand more of your inner, spiritual-self, and operate under that power.

Below are the eight *'Points of Empowerment'* – Make a list of these eight powerful points and place these lists where you can see and read them often. Repeat them and you will find that these concepts will become part of your new belief system and you will have a new perspective on life.

1. We are each responsible for our experiences.
2. Every thought we think is creating our future.
3. Everyone is dealing with the damaging patterns of resentment, criticism, guilt, and self-hatred.
4. These are only thoughts and thoughts can be changed.
5. We need to release the past and *accept* everyone.
6. We do not need to forgive only *accept*. Forgiveness is a judgement.
7. **Self-approval** and **self-acceptance** in the '**NOW**' are the keys to my positive change.
8. The point of power is always in the present moment. **THE NOW!**

Do not just get stuck in your specific problems. Remember there are no such things as problems; only situations that don't yet, have solutions. When you accept these ideas and make them a part of your belief system, you become 'powerful', and the problems (situations) will often solve themselves (solutions). The object is to change what you believe about yourself and the world you live in.

The Problem (Situation)

How many people in the world are suffering from a deep sense of depression and hopelessness? Almost EVERYONE. Some people experience it frequently, others only occasionally. Those who don't seem to experience it at all are usually just bottling it up, refusing to accept their innermost feelings. The root cause of all this depression is that our lives seem to lack true purpose. We have a deep inner knowing that there is more to life than what most of us are experiencing. But the mystical elusive meaning of life appears as a far distant concept. We feel totally hopeless to find it. So we live our lives with that vague but very real sense of discontent ever present. We are told we need to forgive, we read that we need to forgive to find peace.

We try to cover it up with dreams of material success, but we know deep inside that no level of attainment can bring lasting happiness. We look at the rich and famous, the wealthy and successful, and see that most often even they are not satisfied and at peace. But we try to fool ourselves – "If I was them, I would be different, I would be totally happy". Even the people who seem to be looking after themselves, who live simply and are generally happy and enjoying life, still have the same inner feelings of emptiness.

Most often we surround ourselves with as many luxuries as we can afford to distract us from our inner emptiness. But every time we get something new, the satisfaction is only temporary, and we move our hope for happiness onto some future event. And we also know that when we die, we won't take those luxuries with us.

All those years of hard work, all the years of enduring long days filled with anxiety and stress, so that you could eventually drive a nice car, live in a nice house, have a nice TV etc. Of course you could only appreciate those luxuries in the small amount of time off from work, and not during illness, in between moments of pain caused by personal problems, relationships, financial difficulties, loss of loved ones, and all the rest of life's ceaseless string of disturbing events and traumatic experiences. Then your own time of death arrives - were the few moments of luxury worth a lifetime of hardship?

Life doesn't have to be like that, there is a solution. You can have a life of true success, true satisfaction, and true freedom. Or you can keep living in depression, hopelessness, anxiety, doubt, discontentment, suffering and emptiness.

The Choice is Yours

The sooner you realise that *acceptance* and *choice* will set you free, then you will find true happiness, lasting satisfaction, and the real purpose of your life. From childhood we are conditioned to believe that we need to be constantly achieving in order to be happy, so the need to achieve is translated into a never-ending list of future plans and dreams. All these plans and dreams are your way of placing hope for satisfaction in some future event. You will eventually have to *accept* that this is a false hope, for external events never bring lasting inner satisfaction.

So obviously then the only way to achieve true inner satisfaction is to not need anything external to be content. And if you don't need anything external then obviously you must already have exactly what you do need – a mind capable of choosing contentment, a mind capable of *acceptance* and *self-love*, a mind capable of releasing the past. So why should we wait any longer? **Choose it NOW**. Perhaps you will find that you need to keep reminding yourself that satisfaction is accessible to us right now.

Remind yourself of this:

"I CAN be satisfied with my situation right NOW"

Now that you know that satisfaction is only internal and not related to anything external, life becomes EASY. Life is easy but unfortunately for too many people they make it difficult. If your life is not working **CHANGE IT!** Simple! It is so easy to do so, but it is so easy to do nothing!

To support your new satisfaction, you must stop striving for external goals to be happy. This does not mean that life becomes dull, and you can't enjoy luxuries and pleasures. It means that if the pleasure is not immediately available, you remain totally satisfied. Living without the need for plans and dreams, is living simply in the present – being satisfied with whatever you have NOW.

You can look forward to some future event, as long as you realise that the event will not satisfy you any more than you already are. For example, you could look forward to a well-deserved holiday, a new car etc, but remaining aware that it will not add to your inner satisfaction.

Perhaps the planned event will never eventualise, or perhaps it will not be as enjoyable as you had planned. And if it does eventually occur, and it is actually enjoyable, then the enjoyment is still only a fleeting and temporary experience and then you will worry about it ending and life becoming dull again. But there would be no loss of happiness if you had only ever let it be viewed as an event, not a desire for some future life improving experience.

By living in a constant state of satisfaction your enjoyment of everyday simple things will grow deeper. There is no need to cut yourself off from your favourite pleasures. But life gets easier when you cut down on indulging in continuous activities to gratify the sense. Simple eating, simple entertainment, simple comforts bring the greatest inner rewards. If you feel that you are ready to benefit from these, move towards them gradually so as not to suffer withdrawal symptoms and end up just as entwined in the need for sense gratification again.

Happiness has much in common with satisfaction. You can't be truly happy with something. You can only be truly happy. There can be no object attached. As soon as you attach an object to the happiness, it becomes temporary. The same applies to unhappiness. Too many people blame others for making them unhappy. No one person can make you happy or unhappy only yourself can make you truly happy. Whether you are happy with a person, a possession, an achievement, or anything else, you can be sure that sometime in the future it's happy inducing qualities will diminish, and you will seek to find a replacement.

Only by stopping the search for an external object of happiness will you discover the true source of ever-available happiness within. When you can maintain your connection to this happiness continually, it automatically transforms your life into joy. We should all make a habit to be happy – it is not as hard as it sounds.

There is a story involving a man talking to his blind friend. They were repeating a conversation they had often.

> The blind man said "You keep speaking of this thing called light, but I don't understand it. Can you hand me some light so I can touch it?"
>
> His friend replied, "Oh no, you can't touch light"
>   "Oh well I will taste it then" the blind man said
>
> "No, no, you can't taste light!"
>   "Very well then, I will listen to it"
>
> "I'm afraid you can't do that either"
>   "And I suppose I can't smell it either?"
>
> "That's correct"
>   "If you will not prove to me its existence, I refuse to believe in it!"
>
> "I have heard that there is a wise man visiting our town, let us go and visit him, perhaps he can help you understand"

So off they went. Immediately upon hearing the problem, the wise man said, "This man will never be able to understand light in his present condition. But it seems that his blindness can be easily healed through a simple operation."

So the blind man underwent the operation and was finally able to see the light. "I was totally disbelieving in the existence of light, and now I can see it with my own eyes!" he exclaimed.

This story can be likened to society's attitude to spirituality. Most people in our culture are like the blind man, refusing to *accept* spirituality's existence because it is not directly obvious. Yet if we underwent the operation, that is if we made the effort to actually live according to spiritual principles, then we would finally observe its constant influences in our lives.

Many people believe that spirituality is only an escape for the weak, for those people who need to hide from the harsh reality of life and suffering, with inevitable death. I used to have that viewpoint also. But really, I was judging the whole question of spiritual existence by the frustration and doubt, which had risen, through my experience of organised religion.

 Whilst innumerable church leaders have displayed obvious hypocrisy and lack of integrity, and the original messages of most religions' founders have been corrupted or superseded over time, it would be unfair to rule our spiritual existence as being entirely false. If wisdom and truth are what people seek, then an open mind, free of preconceived ideas and judgement, will surely be the most beneficial to you.

The Truth

The soul is here on this planet to learn. It learns through experience. You are experiencing every part of life, from the standard daily activities to the totally unexpected dramas, for your soul to learn. Every single experience, every situation, every difficulty, every accomplishment, every work duty, every activity, it is all being experienced purely for spiritual advancement and growth.

There is nothing you can do in life without affecting your spiritual advancement and growth. Most people are unaware that they are already actively travelling on their spiritual journey and have been since birth. We choose our parents; we choose our experiences. Therefore, there is no one we need to forgive because we chose the lessons and learning this time around. We need to *accept* that fact and release the past and get on with the journey.

If you live in accordance with your soul's harmonious nature, then the learning process of life will be made easier, and life becomes meaningful. At present you are very often unconsciously conflicting with the natural harmony of your soul, thereby separating yourself from it and causing you to live in the confusion of a purely materialistic existence.

The true peace and happiness that we all spend our lives searching for can never be found in the material world. For we really are seeking to reconnect with God (Spirit, the creator, the universal mind). In some of us that desire is not so obvious, but it is always subconsciously present. It is the source of our dissatisfaction and our deepest motive to keep living, but since the final goal is not apparent, we search elsewhere for lower forms of satisfaction to distract us from our sense of aloneness.

Some people get confused because they feel that there is some sort of God-presence in our lives, but if it really exists, why does it not show itself in some way to help us? Well it has shown itself indirectly through the teachings and wisdom of a great number of saints and spiritual teachers throughout history.

But it rarely shows itself directly because we have all been given the privilege of **FREE WILL**. This means that we have a right to choose our thoughts and actions, including the ultimate choice of believing or disbelieving in our Creator. If the Universal Mind was directly obvious, we would have no free will to choose our beliefs.

Even though reconnecting with our source is our motivation and purpose, the simple fact is that most people are unwilling to change their current way of living to become harmonious with their soul. So there is no need for God/Spirit to be present in their lives, until they recognise that their self-centred reality is only bringing them temporary satisfaction.

The universal mind is always aware when a person becomes ready and willing to learn truth and change. So then it ensures that the most suitable teachings become available according to the individual's needs. It is up to each of us to choose to open up and allow ourselves to *accept* truth and live in harmony. The Universal Mind is like an endless ocean. Each one of us is like a single wave, rising up from the ocean. The ocean and the waves are one and the same, even though the waves seem small and insignificant. If the waves became calm, they would merge back into the ocean, discovering their united source. If we live by *acceptance* and according to these ideas, our mind will become calm and we will dissolve back into our source, recognising our oneness with God (Spirit, the Creator).

Right Conduct and Right Action

We need to know that our true nature is harmony. Harmony is felt in life as a sense of positivity and purpose. The alternative of harmony is disharmony. This is felt as a sense of negativity. The basic idea of right conduct and right action is to develop our positive qualities and to cease our negative qualities. It is important not to immediately condemn others or ourselves for our negative qualities – or else we fall back into a state of negativity and judgement.

It is vital to remember that God (*the Source*) always ensures that everything is perfect, all is exactly as it should be. This is not immediately obvious from what we can see around us, but this is because every soul is learning what they need at their own pace. Take my case for example, my abusive childhood was as it should be. From that learning I have turned it around to become an abuse counsellor who can help others to climb out of the 'black hole' they have fallen into. I can shine the light down to help them climb out with empathy and compassion. I have been in that 'black hole' and climbed out. They know that I am not asking them to do something that I haven't already done for myself. I now have the 'tools' to help others.

All negativity in this world is only temporary; we are all slowly moving back to awareness of God (*Spirit, the Creator*).

The physical world can be compared to a stage in God's Play; we are all actors playing our predetermined parts for the benefit of our souls. The whole world, the entire universe, is just as real as the stage in a theatre. All that takes place on our stage is in fact only seemingly real, with God/Spirit and our souls as the audience. Our whole life is like a story made manifest for us to learn. All difficulties are placed in the story by our soul in order for us to learn and seek self-improvement. Without obstacles, we would not become aware of our inner disturbances that leave us vulnerable to disharmony. We need to always remember to approach all situations with *acceptance*, positivity, and trust that 'Spirit' has our best interests at heart.

God/Spirit creates every problem we encounter in life as part of our learning experience. This is true for absolutely every type of problem – illness, accidents, relationships, work problems, any life situation that creates emotional or mental disturbances. Not many people notice that their individual problems are merely the obvious signposts of a larger learning experience. Sometimes we manage to relieve or suppress the obvious symptoms through willpower, medicine or just by ignoring them, depending on the nature of the problem. But the learning experience that created the problem will not have dissolved. It will instead be manifesting different or less obvious symptoms.

God's intention is not just to upset us. It is God's intention for us to become aware of the negative attitudes or quality that has been persistently stopping us from experiencing our natural harmony. We are in effect separating ourselves from our soul. God/Spirit is hoping that our difficulty will point us in the right direction towards ceasing the negativity.

Even if we are being negatively affected by someone else's problems, we can be sure that the situation is in some way present to reflect a negativity problem of our own. Otherwise God would not be allowing us to experience it.

When a problem occurs the best thing, you can do is to look at the situation fully. Look at the events leading to the problem and see if there was a disharmonious attitude or expression of negativity in some way. Look at how the problem may be just one symptom of a continuing series of similar difficulties. By ignoring your lessons, similar problems keep being repeated. God's hope is that the repetitive pattern will allow you to recognise the deeper significance of these difficulties.

If the underlying cause is not immediately apparent, then don't be overly concerned. Occasionally a problem occurs seemingly without a reason in order to test your dedication to right conduct and right action. If you wish you can ask God/Spirit to help clarify the cause. In any case, know that you will be presented with the answer if you remain aware. By releasing your anxiety, you may become aware of it even when you're not consciously thinking about it. Otherwise, no doubt God/Spirit will provide another opportunity for you to learn the same lesson, by creating another similar difficulty for you. 'Spirit' has the Plan, not you.

V

Discussion
FORGIVENESS KEEPS US HOOKED

"Once upon a time I was afraid of letting go
Letting feelings in
My emotions stayed behind a door with no key
Leading with my heart was not for me"
Lyric from song by Barbara Streisand

Ultimately, we must learn to take responsibility for our life and all of its circumstances and situations. We may think this is an unfair attitude. For example, some people have been born into certain conditions such as poverty, hardship and abuse, or wealth and ease, or even physical disabilities. And these extreme conditions may arise at any time during life without any responsibility on the part of the individual.

Do not doubt that this has all been chosen by the soul even before birth – the conditions are exactly what is required for that individual's specially needed lessons. Every single thing that we experience is of our own doing. Negative experiences can only be released through *acceptance* and becoming aware of our lessons and developing harmonious attitudes and qualities. Taking responsibility for our entire life is one of the biggest steps forward we can make on our spiritual path.

*The soul doesn't know holding on,
but the ego doesn't know letting go.*

Sufferers of chronic illnesses may have a hard time *accepting* that they are responsible for their unending suffering. It is very easy to understand – the depressed person thinks "Life is terrible, what is the point of living" and so the body acts as a physical reflection of that thought – a body that does not support the living process.

Remember as we think so we become.
Our thoughts create our reality!

We must be sure not to blame anyone for the difficulties in our lives. This is where I believe that forgiveness keeps us hooked into the past! It does not release us but keeps us hooked. Forgiveness is a judgement – it is laying blame on someone else or ourselves. If as metaphysical counsellors and practitioners we stop using the word forgiveness, if we assisted our clients to see that forgiveness will not release them but instead advised our clients to imagine a big red pen crossing out the word forgiveness every time they see the word or hear the word, and write across this word forgiveness the word **ACCEPTANCE**.

Acceptance will set them free and release them from the past. Acceptance will bring them to a state of understanding that everything is as it should be – Spirit's Plan (God's Plan). Acceptance of others includes giving them the right to choose disharmony and ignorance without criticism and judgement.

Louise Hay states in **LOVE YOURSELF, HEAL YOURSELF, 1990**

> *"As I have said many times, I believe that 'should' is one of the most damaging words in our language. Every time we use it, we are, in effect, saying 'wrong'. Either we are wrong, or we were wrong, or we are going to be wrong. I would like to take the word 'should' out of our vocabulary forever and replace it with the word 'could'. 'Could' gives us choice and we are never wrong"*

I feel exactly the same about the word forgive. I believe that 'forgive' is one of the most damaging words in our language. Every time we use it, we are, in effect, saying that we judge or blame someone or ourselves. Either we are blaming/judging, or we were blamed/judged, or we are going to be blamed/judged. I would like to take the word 'forgive' out of our vocabulary forever and replace it with the word *'Accept* and *Acceptance'*.

Acceptance gives us the ability to release the past, unhook from the emotion, unhook from the pain, and let go.

The following flow chart I feel represents our healing journey.

Our Journey Into Healing

Connections with the Source

Shock at our Birth

Childhood – development of ego self – learn to bury our feelings – defend against lacks, hurts or trauma. Learn limiting beliefs about self. Learn judgements

Expect love to come to us from the outside

Live according to the requirements of outer world:

Adolescence – Search for our role models and wisdom figures

Adult – conflicts and stresses between our inner and outer world, Self sabotage by hurting the inner child

Growing dissatisfaction, our spiritual awakening, change, loss, or crisis

Introvert stage:

Begin our search for healing and our meaning – focus on self-healing

Release of our past, **ACCEPTANCE**, surrender, give over, ego shift

Bringing outer life into harmony with our inner life

Realisation of our real potential – an awakening

Learn self-love & **self-acceptance**

Extrovert stage:

Able and ready to give love unconditionally

Fulfillment, wholeness, excitement – spiritual consciousness

Live according to our spiritual essence (soul)

Reconnect with the Source – One with All

VI

Summary and Conclusions
THE KEYS TO SUCCESSFUL HEALING

"We are concerned, are we not, with the exploration of our inward nature which is very complex. This investigation is really self-education – not to change what is, but to understand what is. What is, is far more important than what should be, The understanding of what we actually are is far more essential than to transcend what we are"

J. Krishnamurti from Letters to the Schools Vol. 2 (1985)

It is important for us to realise that we are spiritual beings having a human experience and we are where we need to be NOW. Our spiritual growth and spiritual healing and learning is our responsibility, and we need to accept the challenges to see and discover ourselves through knowledge, universal wisdom, and unconditional love.

Within us is the vast wealth and prosperity of the Universe. We are one with the universal mind and our higher self and ALL that is. There are no rights, wrongs, mistakes, only lessons and teachings. It is not our place to judge others or ourselves.

We need to give daily thanks for the prosperity and abundance in our lives knowing that we deserve the best and we are willing to **ACCEPT** and receive it NOW.

We need to recognise our TRUTH when we see, hear, or touch it and live by this universal truth. We are one with the Divine thought process within us and we are open to receive creative thoughts and ideas now.

It is my dream that in assisting you to find the keys to your successful healing, you may discover these keys that begin to unlock the suffering that so many of us find ourselves in. The keys have been there all down through the ages and these new ones are designed to fit the present locks we find within. For many of us, for our planet, it is urgent that these keys are used now and hopefully we will never forget how to use them again.

ACCEPTANCE AND UNCONDITIONAL LOVE HEALS ALL...

We need to become **Acceptance** and **Unconditional Love**.

We begin our lives in unity. From there, we distinguish between "I" and "not I". This journey, or stretching of the rubber band of existence, forms a figure eight in which we imagine ourselves to be separate, only to discover that we are one AND separate at the same time. It's a paradox, in that the mind cannot solve it, yet the heart can intuit and feel the truth of it.

Unconditional Love

Love is the *Law of Spirit/God*. You live that you may *'learn'* to Love.

You *'love'* that you may learn to *'live'*. No *'other'* lesson is required of humankind.

> What is this 'energy' called out as 'love'? Is it a natural instinct that we have inborn in our genetics? Is it a 'learned' behaviour that we have become programmed and conditioned with.

It is a *feeling* reflected back in a lover's eye, and your lover's affectionate gaze. **Love** is Spirit's force channelled through all these ways and means. The love a mother demonstrates for her child is a different love than what is between two lovers, different still is the love between friends, love between neighbours and spiritual companions.

On and on the many lights filled facets of love.

> This **love** force is represented by various vibrations of **Light**.

As a clairvoyant who literally 'sees' light waves and vibrations, I have learned to 'discern' quite a bit of what I perceive into very organised forms and patterns. Soft pinks and greens floating between lover's hearts is a different love than the high blues and clean yellow flowing between church gathering. None the less the light of love is 'flowing'.

How aware we are of our flow and what we are exchanging with others, the quantity and the quality depends on your awareness level of the subtle energies and the truths they represent. Ignorance of these subtle energies will truly leave you in the dark when it comes to understanding and discernment. Like any creative action, knowledge, wisdom, discernment, and intention are **'key'** components to success in understanding the human energy field and energy vibrations.

Losing 'sight' and understanding of our 'light', will many times send a soul 'searching' ignorantly for substitutes for the true nourishing, uplifting, growth are your 'issues', your fears, your concerns, and opportunities for growth, evolution, consciousness, and awareness.

As within, so without will again be reflected.

When you begin to allow the inner light of your higher self and true soul essence it's voice, sound, and light, you truly begin to live as a **spiritual being** within *God's Will*.

Like lovers 'in love' you will experience a relationship with your 'heart' self. Every time you have a kind thought, utter a kind word, are in service or of service to someone in kindness, you are living the divine principal of unconditional love, and your light grows and expands. You are learning light/vibration, and this can never be stimulating loving vibrations that are lacking and/or missing. These false substitutes of loving vibrations often take the form of addictions, behavioural and chemical.

Sexual, chemical, behavioural (eating, shopping, sports, fantasy thinking, obsessions etc.) addictions are some of love's false inauthentic replacements.

When we begin to recognise the *'light'* of love within our selves, and allow and encourage it to flow unimpeded, it will be easier to recognise loving vibrations in other's reflecting back to us these truths.

The chakra system is a very truthful *mirror* of love vibrations and other energetic patterns. There are 72,000 nadis (channel of life-force energy) in the body, and there are various nerve centres where these channels meet. The Human body has 109 such centres, also called Chakras.

When the chakras are holding powerful, stable clockwise patterns (in general) you are in flow, you are allowing, you are in a non-dominating/controlling state of mind/aura. Whatever is blocking and/or dominating the healthy loving flow of clockwise patterns taken from you, for it is now a part of your soul and its evolution. Once again, your new loving vibrations will be *mirrored* back to you in your life's circumstances.

Soon, you will begin to see your world through loving eyes, feel, taste, smell the beauty and joy in all things. In essence, you experience *heaven on earth.*

As each of us cultivates and grow our gardens in love, not only is our own light/vibrations enriched, but we are also able to pass these loving vibrations on and on to every life we touch, like one candle lighting and illuminating another.

"You take all the 'Love' with you".

So, you see love is so far-reaching that is transcends physical death. As in the movie 'Ghost' our main character (Patrick Swayze) as he was ascending into the light after physically dying said *"You take all the 'Love' with you"*.

True unadulterated love is never jealous, possessive, nor does it have 'conditions'. Everything, and everyone blooms in the light of love. As we re-incarnate life after life, we come in to learn and grow in the lessons of love, see it manifest in the unlimited ways in the many different circumstances we have 'chosen' to experience.

Love is the strongest most healing guiding 'force' in the Universe. As an energy healer, I know that what truly 'heals' my clients is love and its many colourful vibrations. Love and its many prismatic facets, re-knits, re-kindles, re-forms and re-builds the fabric of the soul's vibrations that I have the privilege of touching and healing in the most loving, caring ways and means I know in the moment.

Touching in love is not limited to trained Healers. Any time you touch someone with permission in a caring, emotionally loving **'heartfelt'** manner, you too are a 'healer' and bring the light and vibration of the most powerful force known to another.

Live life, love life, and I wish you all an **'abundance'** of the healing, life affirming energies known as **'love'**.

Beginners Advice - On Healing

From my own experience I found that when first starting in the field of 'healing' and a family member was hurt or ill... I would extract all their pain and heal them... but I placed it within me... and I took the pain or the illness...

Thankfully I learned pretty quickly how *not to do that* and made the changes necessary to become a giver not a receiver.

Now I no longer extract anything.... all I do is become the extension cord. Hollow Bones. One end is plugged into Source/the Creator (*from where I believe that all healing energy comes from*), and the other end is plugged into the person receiving... allowing the Healing energy to flow, freely without expectations or control. That way I do not take anything from the person and it is truly up to the individual and their connection to their Creator God/dess of their understanding to accept the extra boost of Healing Energy and to affect their own Healing Process.

As for treating family and close friends we do have a soul connection, physical connection, and karma history... But why burden oneself with a lot of extra's... keeping the healing as simple as possible... because of our Love for the person there tends to be a greater connection, so we tend to feel what they are experiencing. It is important to stay detached from them while you are giving them the Healing Energy.... if we can see ourselves as only a vessel for the energy to flow from, it may help in keeping ourselves detached. It is almost the same as not allowing Doctors to operate on family members.

One thing that I also do, when I receive a message in my body of pain, and I know it is not mine... I turn around and thank it for bringing the attention and awareness to me, but that it truly is not mine, so I ask it to leave.

(You can rest assured, if it is not yours it leaves... if it is yours, it stay's)

Then one would have to ask, why did this pain come into my body? It could only be there so that you can recognise the location for you to send healing to...
Again it can become complicated...

When one steps out of the way, works without expectation or control of what you think it should be doing or what you think etc...

Imagine a life where your worth is not determined by external validation, but by your own intrinsic value. Release the suffocating pressure of expectations and finding joy in simple, meaningful contributions.

Change the thoughts and become the river... flow with it and allow the Person and the Creator to do the work...
Step aside, let go, and let God. Be the servant...

So, in a nutshell:
Detach, let go, and honour the pain that is not yours, release. When sending healing energy, become hollow bones, be like the extension cord or the river, and allow it to flow freely. Stop taking it in or pulling it out... just give.

Happiness is a Conscious Choice

Happiness is not a destination to be reached, but a continuous practice of perspective and **intention**. By understanding that our interpretation of events matters more than the events themselves, we gain the ultimate psychological freedom, the ability to choose our response, regardless of circumstances.

This is your permission slip to live authentically, to be gloriously, unapologetically yourself. Because in the end, the only approval that truly matters is your own.

Our conscious mind, the ego, holds the events, memories, and emotions experienced in this lifetime. Our subconscious mind has that information, plus information from other lifetimes, dimensions, and realities. Our conscious mind often denies any past life or dimensional information as we first become aware of it and is rarely aware of our issues.

Our issues (*situations*) are the conditions we placed on love in the past and are still dealing with today. Our issues are what we did not understand in past lives and include similar things we do not understand in this life. They make it challenging for us to have **unconditional love** for ourselves and unconditional compassion for others.

What we did not master in the past is drawn to us in this lifetime. Our subconscious mind re-creates these issues over and over by using our energy to attract new people and situations to us who reflect these issues. One of the most important realisations we have is: Our Higher Self, working through our subconscious mind, wants us to realise **we are creating our reality** with each of our **choices** – and – we have many **choices**.

This realisation gives us a greater understanding of the **choices** we make and allows us the freedom to create what we desire in our lives without old patterns energetically affecting us. Each of us can do this. We quickly become aware that we have many **choices** about how we react (or not react) to each situation, each moment, in our lives.

You did the best you could with what you knew at the time. Don't let new wisdom lead you to condemn yourself over old struggles.

Accept yourself and move forward.

The Keys to Successful Healing are:

ACCEPTANCE, CHOICE, and
UNCONDITIONAL LOVE.

Knowledge and **attitude** are the true keys to **freedom, peace,** and **happiness.** We are all capable of knowing much more about our past, our future, and ourselves than we realise. Secrets about our inner complexity - which is at the core of how we interpret and deal with life - remain secrets only because we have not sought the truth or have refused to acknowledge it and grow accordingly when faced with it.

Each of us, however, can become empowered to change our attitudes, recreate ourselves, and take control of our lives and our fates. Spirit is within us, in our thoughts, hearts, and souls. **Freewill is always at work,** by omission or commission, and is the main factor in determining our fate.

After all, it is via freewill that we interpret every situation, and interpreting situations as empowering opens the door to higher creativity and better decision-making. And each of us is a Creator, every second of every day.

Being a part of Nature, we also experience cycles, and the ups and downs we go through are natural and necessary for reflection and growth. Accordingly, nothing we experience is in vain, though we may forget or fail to understand this at times of stress and confusion. In essence, everything is leading us, collectively and individually, **toward higher consciousness**, one way or another, moment by moment, heartbeat by heartbeat.

We benefit most, as does our world, when we **consciously participate** in this movement towards higher consciousness.

What I have learned is that no matter how difficult things seem, there is always hope.
Plus I've learned that no matter how powerless we feel or how horrible things seem, we can't give up. We have to keep going. Even when it's scary, even when all of our strength seems gone, we have to keep picking ourselves back up and moving forward, because whatever we're battling in the moment, it will pass, and we will make it through. We've made it this far. We can make it through whatever comes next.

Embracing Acceptance

The key to happiness lies in not resisting what is. True peace comes from accepting each moment as it unfolds, regardless of our preferences, judgments, or desires.

Reality is simply what is happening right now. It is neither good nor bad—it just is. The moment we embrace this truth instead of fighting it, we free ourselves from fear and suffering.

So meet each moment with unconditional love, compassion, and wisdom. Let go of rigid expectations about how things *should* be, as they only create unnecessary struggle. Instead, align yourself with reality, and you will find true freedom and happiness.

I now want to introduce you to some excellent **tools** for your 'healing toolbox'.

TOOLS FOR YOUR HEALING TOOLBOX
OTHER TECHNIQUES OF HEALING

Empathic Healing

We are conduits of power, when we have dams inside the body (energy blocks) the energy cannot be released. Try to teach your body to release and to become a river! Visualise a solid gold rod about one (1) inch in diameter going out the top of your head seven (7) inches and straight down into the ground about 50 feet. This will begin to ground out the pain until you can re-teach your body not to hold onto pain.

Green Healing Light

This is a visualisation to heal every time you use your hands. It is simple. Begin by relaxing and centring your mind, body, and spirit in your heart chakra. Next, visualise a beautiful ball of green light spinning clockwise in your chest or heart chakra. Now, visualise this green light flowing into your shoulders, elbows, wrists, and hands. Now visualise it flowing into your hips, knees, ankles, and feet. Now visualise a seven (7) inch sphere of green light forming around every joint in your body.

You have just connected your heart chakra to all of your secondary chakras. Your hands have all always been your primary healing tools. Every time your body has been hurt, your hands immediately hold the area, and it feels better. You are unconsciously running heart energy down your arms into your hands and healing your body. Everybody is a healer!

For wonderful grounding, visualise a ball of red light at the base of your spine, then visualise it flowing first, into all of your skeleton lighting up each bone like a fluorescent tube with bright red light, then all of the muscles in your body lit up with bright red light!

Physio-Emotional Release Therapy – P.E.R.T. ©

P.E.R.T. was developed in Australia by Natural Therapists & Counsellors **Greg Fitzgerald** and **Ann Williams-Fitzgerald**. It consists of a vibrational energy-based and counselling therapy for the releasing of structural and subtle energy blockages stored in the body and the auric field.

P.E.R.T. allows the client to

RELEASE, REPAIR & RENEW

P.E.R.T. is a complete holistic system that addresses the **'whole'** client on the four vibrational levels: - Emotional, Mental, Spiritual and Physical to initiate transformational healing at the clients' pace – we call this *core* healing – or *Physio-Emotional Release*.

What we would call *core healing* happens in the healing process, after a great deal of psychological and energetic work has been done. P.E.R.T. is pure energy releasing, shifting, and transforming on a very deep core level. Being trained in many modalities helps to open things up from the top, making it easier for the foundation to shift and leaving less *'rubble or weeds'* to deal with when the change happens.

We liken P.E.R.T. to *'preparing the soil and weeding the garden.'* The weeds are our emotional blockages – past hurts, traumas, and pain.

P.E.R.T. is another path of healing therapy - when a person is determined to tread the pathway to healing, however difficult it is, and is willing to invest time and energy into their healing process, then they can with the assistance of a P.E.R.T.

AN EXERCISE IN P.E.R.T.

Step One- Write a List
Any event or person who has hurt or upset you as far back as you can remember.

Step Two- Write a List
Anything you have done that you feel guilty about!!! Now after each item listed write:-

"I **Accept** myself and let go"

Step Three- Write Letters to:
Mother, Father, Grandfather, Children, Husband, Wife, Ex's, Brothers, Sisters, workers, boss, friends, etc. Anyone who needs to be released.

Step Four- Write three letters to Self:
1. Little self (boy or girl) inner child
2. Abused Self
3. Self now.

Note:
With the letters, always start with the negative emotions first and always end on a positive.

You need be able to **accept**. Be able to let go and set yourself completely free and set the other person free.

Step Five - Write a List

List all illness or accidents that you have ever had.
Also list the month and year that you had those illnesses / accidents etc. Now look at this list of illnesses, accidents and dis-ease and then look at what was happening in your life around the same time as these listed illnesses etc.

Important: **DON'T READ THE LETTERS AFTER WRITING THEM.**

Place them into envelopes and seal them up. Now set aside some time to burn these envelopes and release the energetic ties. As the smoke rises to 'Spirit' feel the release within your own body. Once burnt take the ashes and bury them in the earth to ground the energy.

A Guide for Checking Your Boundaries Within Relationships

Without Good Boundaries
Feel afraid - anticipate crisis - always expect the worst to happen
Have difficulty saying "no"
Change your behaviour, plans or opinions to pacify partner - withhold your truty
Make exceptions and excuses for partner's behaviour - even when appropriate
Are unclear about your choices, preferences, and opinions - wonder if you are right often
Make others responsible for your good and bad feelings about yourself
Use guilt, fear, shame, intimidation, or interrogation in attempting to change partner
Are more focused on partner's needs, emotions, and feelings than you are on your own
Are unable to get angry but often feel victimised
Feel you must physically separate to get space and feel safe
Often discount intuitive hunches
Will comply with unwanted sexual advances in order to feel loved
Attempt to get your own needs met by constantly doing for others
Avoid knowing the truth in attempting to avoid pain

With Good Boundaries
Feel secure - grounded - able to cope
Are able to set limits and say "no"
Remain true to self and attempt mutually satisfying compromise that respects the needs of both
Is flexible and accountable and expect others to be flexible and accountable also
Feel clear and decisive and act to get what you want and need
Take responsibility for your own feelings and responses
Speak with "I" messages and attempt to hear and understand partner
Are in touch with your own needs, emotions, feelings and attend to them with self nurturing
Can express healthy anger and refuse to be victimised
Can stay engaged and yet feel separate
Listen and abide by intuition
Do not compromise your integrity for sex
Are direct about getting needs met and does not attempt to manipulate others
Willing to experience temporary frustration or pain as an accepted part of growth

Total up your score: If you have seven (7) points or more on the "Without Good Boundaries" side, you will know this is an issue affecting you or your relationships.

True empowerment emerges not from controlling external circumstances, but from taking radical responsibility for our internal landscape. By **accepting** that our happiness is an internal **choice**, not a result of external conditions, we liberate ourselves from victim mentality. Every challenge becomes an opportunity, every setback a potential breakthrough.

SPIRITUAL MIND TREATMENT

A Spiritual Mind Treatment is affirmative prayer.

What is affirmative prayer? It is a prayer that declares a spiritual Truth. For example, when Jesus the Christ spoke the Word, his healing statement was declared with great power and conviction. He didn't say, "Oh please, God, let Lazarus be healed." He said, "Lazarus, come forth!" (John 11:43)

A Spiritual Mind Treatment, or affirmative prayer, is *"a recognition of Spirit's Omniscience, Omnipotence, and Omnipresence, and a realization of humanity's unity with Spirit..."* (Ernest Holmes, Science of Mind textbook, pg. 149)

SPIRITUAL MIND TREATMENT

Step 1: Recognition

We begin every Spiritual Mind Treatment with Recognition that there is One Life, and that Life is God. You may call God by any other name that makes it clear and personal to you, such as: Spirit, Universe, The Creator, Allah, Buddha, Infinite Mind, the One, the Force, Light, or any other term that feels real to you.

Begin with a statement recognising God, such as: "I know there is an Infinite Spirit that I call the Universe." or "I recognise the One as the power, the presence, and the love of All That Is."

Step 2: Unification

In the Unification step of Spiritual Mind Treatment, we affirm that the same Spirit that God is, we are. We are OF God - Divine emanations. Since God is all there is, there can be nothing outside of God, and no one separate from God. And so we realise and declare our Oneness as spiritual beings.

After you do the above Recognition step, make some simple declaration of your unity with the Allness of God, such as: "I know that I am One with that Infinite Mind." Or "I recognise my unity with All That Is."

Step 3: Realisation

In Step 3 of your Spiritual Mind Treatment, you want to Realise the qualities or attributes of God/Spirit which you want to embrace within yourself - to call forth in your own consciousness. These are the Divine qualities inherent within you which want to become more conscious OF.

And so you might want to say something like, "I know that the Divine qualities of peace, power, plenty, and wisdom are already within me. I embrace them now."

Or "All that God is, I AM. I step forth my true Divinity, saying yes to my own prosperity, guidance, order, harmony, and love."

Step 4: Thanksgiving

Step 4 of your Spiritual Mind Treatment is Thanksgiving. An attitude of gratitude is essential to establishing a new intention in our lives. In giving thanks, we are declaring that it is already done. We are grateful for it. It is so.

In your Thanksgiving step, you may want to say something like "I am so grateful for the revelation of this spiritual Truth in my life." Or "It is with great gratitude that I accept this transformation of consciousness for myself."

Step 5: Release

In Step 5, the Release step of your Spiritual Mind Treatment, you let go and let God. You are turning your affirmative declaration of Truth entirely over to Infinite Love, Spirit, the Allness that is God. It is a very important step, because as long as you hold on to it, nothing can take place.

You may want to simply say, "I release. I let go. I let the Spirit do It's perfect work." Or "I trust the Universe to provide for me. It is done. It is so." Or "And so it is! Amen."

The Three I's

A Spiritual Precept
© 1994 Ann Williams-Fitzgerald PhD

Integrity - *Intention* - *Intuition*

The **Three I's** is truly a wonderful precept to live by. Not only in your spiritual life but also in every aspect of your day to day lives. No matter what it is you are considering doing, check in first with your **Three I's** and see if you get a tick on all three areas. Ask yourself "Am I in **integrity** with this action? Am I infringing on others and I letting others infringe on me", "What are my **intentions?** Are they pure or am I flattering my ego?" "What does my intuition tell me? Does my gut tell me it's the right action". If you can not get *three* ticks to all your questions. **DON'T DO IT!**

You need to have three ticks before you proceed ahead with the action you were considering regardless of whether we are talking about healings, counselling, dealing with clients, staff, or family members. Applying for a new job or deciding on a course of action. This simple but very important precept can be effectively used in every and all areas of your life. Only you can actively work with the **Three I's** as no one else can tell you what Integrity, Intention or Intuition means to you. This is a very effective and very personal precept to activate and use in your life. If you truly live by the **Three I's** you will find huge energy shifts taking place in your life.

No matter what workshop I facilitate, whether it is Reiki, Spiritual Healing, Seichim, Psychic Development, Crystals or Stress Management, I always introduce to my students or clients the precept of the **Three I's** for their growth. I welcome you to embrace the **Three I's** and see the difference in your life it will make.

Integrity

No infringement on others or allowing others to infringe on you.
Not imposing your will on others or allowing
others to impose their will on you.
Being honest with yourself.

Intention

Your intent must be pure - no ego involved.
Earnest in your intentions.
Right conduct

Intuition

Trust your Inner Self - your insight, your guidance
Your gut feeling must be giving you the OK.
Your Yes/No centre is in place. Checking In with yourself -
Does it feel right.
Direct perception of your truths.
The ability to perceive your own truths.
To walk your walk and talk your talk.

Overview of The Three I's

Integrity

No infringement on others or allowing others to infringe on you.
Not imposing your will on others or allowing
others to impose their will on you.
Being honest with yourself.

The Key to Integrity

Be at peace with your past by accepting yourself now. Honour your principles and walk with dignity. Integrity is a quality that reflects a position of being sound or whole. It denotes an acceptance of your innate goodness and virtue.

Shadow Side - Betrayal

Those who betray others, delude themselves. They deny the truth. Betrayal is an activity that reflects dishonesty. It is based on deception and disloyalty to self. You are repressed by fear; you are intimidated by your true feelings.

Intention

*Your intent must be pure - no ego involved.
Earnest in your intentions.
Right conduct*

Key to Intention

Before you perform any task, know your true intent.
Those who know their intentions are mindful of their purpose.
Their focus remains sharp, and their actions are impeccable.
Intention is a state of mind that reflects your motivations.
It indicates your priorities and expectations.

Shadow Side – Distraction

Distraction brings disorder and causes confusion. You become lost in a world of delusion. Distraction is an activity that reflects an inability to be disciplined. It is based on a lack of perseverance and an absence of focus.

Intuition

Trust your Inner Self - your insight, your guidance
Your gut feeling must be giving you the OK.
Your Yes/No centre is in place. Checking In with yourself -
Does it feel right?
Direct perception of your truths.
The ability to perceive your own truths.
To walk your walk and talk your talk.

Key to Intuition

Practice silencing your rational mind and attune to your feelings. Surrender any judgements or negative thinking. Your intuition opens you to truth. A gateway to enlightenment is revealed. Intuition is a faculty that enables you to acquire instinctive knowledge. It bypasses the rational mind and its conscious reasoning.

Shadow Side – Confusion

With an overloaded mind there is no place to rest. You stand at the crossroads, confused by your quest. Confusion is a state that reflects internal conflict. It denotes an inability to assimilate information easily. Confusion blocks your imagination and hinders your growth.

CLOSURE

This book has been waiting to go to print, but for some reason I still felt something was missing. But I was not sure what it was, and then it suddenly dawned on me while driving that what was missing, was I still did not have my closure, that release and completion was somehow needed.

So in January 2000, I found myself heading to Tasmania, to affect what I will term that 'closure' to this my healing journey. I decided that this would be a road trip, so I set off on my journey to drive from Mackay in North Queensland to Hobart in Tasmania.

I found it was necessary to go back to my birth home to lay my ghosts to rest. I realised that I could not achieve this from Queensland – this journey was vital to my healing. I found I needed to go to certain areas, meet with certain people so that I could release myself energetically from the past – to cut the energy cords so to speak.

I spent time with my sister, I made peace with the land and the karmic ties it had with me. I spent a wonderful afternoon with an uncle and cousin who made me feel welcome and part of the family – this will be a special memory. I had reconnected with family I had not seen for many years.

The one thing that became obvious to me, while I was in Tasmania, was the way being there had affected me, I would often find myself feeling sad and faraway for most of the time. It was like a dark cloud would descend on me. Hard to explain but easy to feel.

As I left Tasmania to head home to Mackay, I felt deep inside that it might be the last time that I would see Tasmanian shores, but as I watched the shore fade from sight, I also felt a lightness return to my soul (my essence). I had made my peace, and now I only look forward to my guiding light .... my healing journey now had closure.

"I am, the I am that I am"

"I am, the I am that I am"

"I am, the I am that I am"

"I am a part of all that is".

Ann

The Prayer of St Francis

Lord, make me an instrument of your peace;
where there is hatred, let me sow love;
where there is injury, pardon;
where there is doubt, faith;
where there is despair, hope;
where there is darkness, light;
and where there is sadness, joy.

O Divine Master,
grant that I may not so much seek to be consoled as to console;
to be understood, as to understand;
to be loved, as to love;
for it is in giving that we receive,
it is in pardoning that we are pardoned,
and it is in dying that we are born to Eternal Life.

Amen.

Bibliography

Atreya 1976
    PRANA - THE SECRET OF YOGIC HEALING
    York Beach, ME, USA: Samuel Weiser Inc

Baker, Dr. Douglas 1975
    ESOTERIC HEALING
    Essendon, Herts, UK: Douglas Baker

Foundation for Inner Peace 1975
    A COURSE IN MIRACLES
    Coleman Graphics, Farmingdale, NY USA

Gray, John, PhD 1994
    WHAT YOU FEEL, YOU CAN HEAL
    Heart Publishing Co, Mill Valley, CA USA

Hay, Louise 1984
    YOU CAN HEAL YOUR LIFE
    Hay House, Santa Monica CA USA

Hay, Louise 1990
    LOVE YOURSELF, HEAL YOURSELF
    Hay House, Santa Monica CA USA

Sommer, Charles 1992
    LICKING YOUR WOUNDS
    Devorss Publication, Marina del Ray, CA USA

Sommer, Charles 1995
    THE NEXT STEP WITH SPIRIT
    Devorss Publication, Marina del Ray, CA USA

Roman, Sanaya 1997
    SOUL LOVE
    HJ Kramer Inc, Tiburon. CA USA

About the Author

Ann Williams-Fitzgerald Ph.D., Author, Independent Reiki Master Teacher Trainer & Metaphysical practitioner did return to Tasmania in 2019 after spending 40 years in North Queensland and now resides in the Tamar Valley in Northern Tasmania, Australia with her husband, *Greg Fitzgerald*, and their rescue cat Hamish.

Ann was born in Tasmania in 1953 and moved to Queensland in 1980. Ann has a wide experience of life on many levels; Ann's search for *'spiritual truth'* started at the age of 9 years, when Ann realised that not everyone was capable of having clear visions. She had taken it for granted that, all little girls had dreams about things that later happened. Ann has over 33+ years' experience in metaphysics and healing work. Ann has a Ph.D. in Metaphysics and a PhD in Philosophy of Counselling & Spiritual Healing, Master of Contemporary Arts (Visual) and is the author of three books, five card decks and has written for numerous magazines in Australia and overseas. Ann is a full member of the Australian Society of Authors (ASA).

Ann has been channeling **'Son of White Cloud'** (a Native American) and others now for over 31 years. Ann and Greg have travelled extensively teaching workshops and working quietly within the healing field in UK, Canada, USA, and Australia. Ann has always known that all knowledge is within us. When we are in touch with our inner selves, we automatically become in touch with our guides.

She sees her life as a journey of self-discovery and has for many years pursed various methods of self-development in order to achieve an understanding of herself and others. Ann has been reading Tarot for over 44 years both here in Australia and Overseas, Ann has helped many of her clients find their true path in life. Over many years she has acquired a following that literally spans the globe. Her repeat clients are a testament to her incredibly accurate readings.

Ann is also a Professional and Spiritual Counsellor (who holds a Diploma of Professional Counselling from the Australian Institute of Professional Counsellors).

Ann is credited with teaching and coining the phrase The Three I's (3 I's), being:

'I' for Integrity, 'I' for Intention and 'I' for Intuition.

In 1988, Ann, one of the innovators in Australia to market the concept of bright and inviting 'New Age Gift' stores, set up in Mackay, the first of her seven stores in the successful retail chains called 'The Mystic Connection', 'Rainforest Magic' & 'BE Green'. Ann sold the last and original Mackay outlet in April 2000. In the past 25 years, Ann felt drawn away from retailing and the business world, to concentrate on teaching, writing, healing, and offering guidance to those who seek her out.

Her motto now is simply:
Love All, Serve All - Help Ever, Hurt Never.
(From Sathya Sai Baba)

Ann's conviction that there are like-minded people who have a need to come together on a regular basis for fellowship and healing, prompted her to establish *Eagle Lodge Spiritual Centre* in Mackay, North Queensland in 1994 and there are over a dozen Eagle Lodge Spiritual groups around Australia continuing her vision.

Ann is available for workshops in *Australia and overseas.* Ask yourself what one step you could take now that would contribute the most to your spiritual path. Then take it and reach out! Learn to *Trust, Play and Sing* with the *Universe and Spirit.*

Ann Williams-Fitzgerald PhD

Auz Vizions
14 Mary St, George Town,
Tasmania 7253 Australia
E-mail: annwf@mac.com

http://www.innerwisdom.com.au
https://anniefitz.com.au/

Mobile 0417 602 822

www.ingramcontent.com/pod-product-compliance
Lightning Source LLC
Chambersburg PA
CBHW020544080526
44583CB00013B/990